Pedro Loves Saving the Planet

STAY SAFE!

Looking after the planet is great fun if you follow these guidelines:

- Wear gloves when picking up trash.

- Wear a helmet when cycling and always ask a grown-up to come with you.

Brimming with creative inspiration, how-to projects, and useful information to enrich your everyday life, quarto.com is a favorite destination for those pursuing their interests and passions.

Consultant: Ben Ballin
Designer: Mike Henson
Commissioning Editor: Emily Pither
Editor: Victoria Garrard
Creative Director: Malena Stojić
Associate Publisher: Rhiannon Findlay

First published in 2023 by Happy Yak, an imprint of The Quarto Group.
100 Cummings Center, Suite 265D
Beverly, MA 01915, USA.
T (978) 282-9590 F (978) 283-2742
www.quarto.com

A CIP record for this book is available from the Library of Congress.

ISBN 978-0-7112-6777-0
eBook ISBN 978-0-7112-6776-3

Manufactured in Guangdong, China TT122022

9 8 7 6 5 4 3 2 1

MIX
Paper from responsible sources
FSC® C016973
FSC www.fsc.org

JESS FRENCH

DUNCAN BEEDIE

Pedro Loves Saving the Planet

I'm Buzz, the bumblebee. Look out for me buzzing around Pedro and his friends!

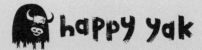

HELLO, I'M PEDRO, I LOVE OUR PLANET.
Isn't it incredible? It's called Earth. It is just
one of many planets, but it is our home.

Earth is
BEE-utiful!

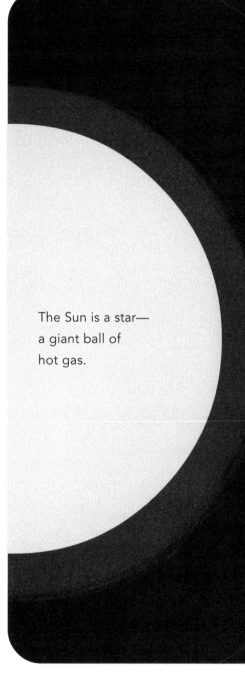

The Sun is a star—
a giant ball of
hot gas.

We think Earth is the only planet
that can support life so it's
important we look after it and
protect it from harm.

Earth moves around the Sun, along with other planets. Together, they are known as the solar system.

Planets are big lumps of rock that move around stars.

From space, Earth looks blue! That's because its surface is mostly covered with water.

Everything we do affects the plants and animals around us, so it's important to make the right decisions to protect our world. That's why I joined my school's eco club.

My brother Daniel loves to tell me things about our incredible planet...

...such as how a blanket of gases keep it at just the right temperature.

Heat from the Sun
The rays of the Sun warm up Earth. Without something to keep it in, the heat would disappear and the planet would get too cold.

Some sunrays enter the atmosphere, bouncing off Earth. Some escape into space. And others are trapped within the atmosphere.

THE ATMOSPHERE

A cozy blanket
The atmosphere acts like a blanket, keeping the heat in. It makes Earth snug and warm—perfect for animals and plants.

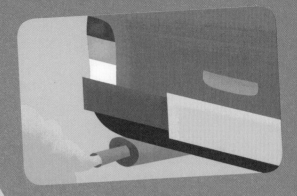

Greenhouse gases
When we burn gasoline and coal, we create gases called greenhouse gases.

The extra greenhouse gases trap in more heat and Earth starts to get too warm for the plants and animals. This is called global warming.

Too much heat isn't good for me.

Protect the planet!
Global warming is very bad for the planet. One of the best ways to prevent it is for people to stop burning gasoline and coal.

We're on our way to visit my eco club's new cabin. I can't wait to see it!

My teacher has challenged us all to travel in a way that won't harm our planet. Daniel and I are going to walk. I wonder how everyone else will arrive.

GETTING AROUND

There are all sorts of ways of getting from A to B. Some are better for the planet than others.

Vehicles that run on gasoline or diesel release nasty fumes, which are damaging to the planet.

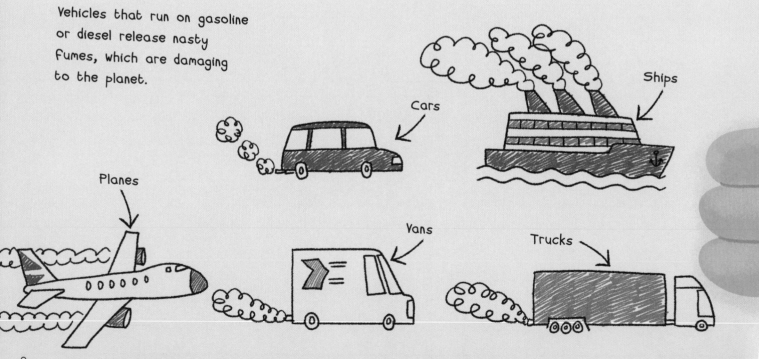

Cars

Ships

Planes

Vans

Trucks

Vehicles that carry lots of passengers are less damaging to the planet because the pollution is shared between many people.

If you have to travel in a vehicle that runs on gasoline or diesel, try to share the journey with as many people as possible!

Lots of buses are now electric!

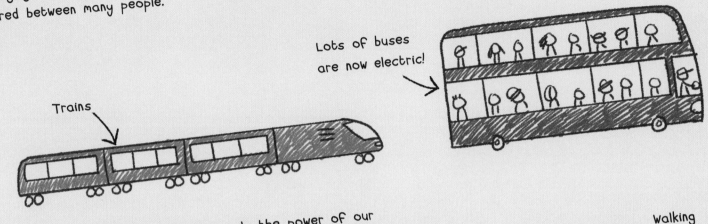

Trains

Lots of ways to get around use only the power of our incredible bodies so they hardly damage the planet at all.

Walking

Scooters

Bikes

Vehicles that are powered by electricity can be better for the planet as they don't release dangerous fumes.

Electric car

ANIMAL RESCUE CENTER

Electric Car

"Hi Pedro. We are charging our electric car. It runs on electricity instead of burning fuel."

Electric cars are plugged in to recharge—a bit like a phone or a tablet.

Doesn't release harmful gases.

Makes very little noise when it is driven.

Can take hours to charge up the battery.

"I love your bike, Bella!"

"Thanks! We've had such a fun ride. It's so much easier to see bugs from my bike than it is from the car!"

"And it's so much kinder to the planet, too."

Wow! The eco cabin looks fantastic.

It has walls covered in plants,

Plants take in greenhouse gases and help clean the air.

solar panels on the roof,

Solar panels make electricity from the Sun's rays.

and straw insulation!

Insulation acts like a blanket around the cabin. It keeps the inside warm.

When can I move in?

We use electricity for lots of different things: to switch on our light bulbs, to charge our phones, and to power our televisions. But where does electricity come from?

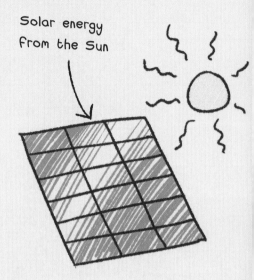

Solar energy from the Sun

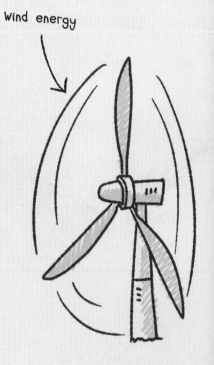

Wind energy

Renewable Energy

Electricity can be made in lots of different ways. Some ways are renewable, which means they can be used again and again.

Non-renewable Energy

Some energy is non-renewable, which means it can only be used once.

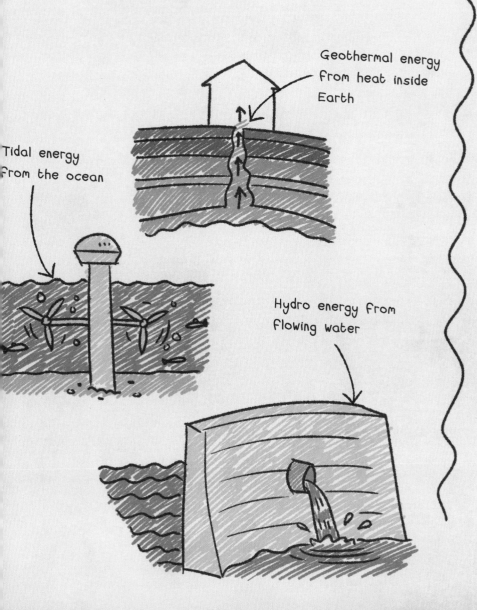

Geothermal energy from heat inside Earth

Tidal energy from the ocean

Hydro energy from flowing water

Gas

Coal

Oil →

"There is plenty of room for local wildlife to make their homes here at our cabin. This swift box will make a great nest for a family of swifts."

"I can't wait for bats to come and roost in our bat box."

"This log pile will attract beetles, woodlice, and earwigs."

You lot are buzzing with ideas!

"This rain barrel will collect rainwater, which we can use to water plants."

Water is precious. It's really important to use it carefully...

Water doesn't have to come straight from the tap. If you're not going to drink it, water can come from all sorts of places and can be recycled (used again).

We can use these buckets of rainwater to water the garden.

This leftover water can give our house plants a drink.

For some things, you do need to use water from the tap but you can limit the amount of water you use. Here are some ideas:

Always turn the tap off while you are brushing your teeth.

Instead of waiting for the tap to run cold for a drink of water, fill a jug and put it in the fridge to cool.

Add fresh fruit for a tasty twist!

If you can, use a dishwasher instead of washing up by hand.

Eat more vegetables!

Meat takes lots of water to produce so encourage your family to try meat-free recipes.

Inside the cabin, everything is made of materials that are sustainable or recycled.

If you can make something again and again without the materials being used up, it is sustainable.

This glass comes from old jars and bottles!

Bee-utiful!

These curtains are made of recycled cotton.

These plant pots are made from a used aluminum can, an old cup, and an old boot!

New trees have been planted in the forest that gave us the wood for this table.

The plates are made of bamboo. New bamboo plants will grow really quickly.

These chairs were once soda bottles!

20

This is our pledge tree. Later we are going to write down our pledges for saving the planet.

"First we need to cut out the paper leaves."

"What should we do with the leftover paper?"

The Seven Rs are a great way to figure out what to do with your waste. Look, they are on our poster...

THE SEVEN Rs

We humans love stuff but making it uses a lot of energy and throwing it away can damage our planet. So, before asking your parents to buy you something, or throwing your old stuff away, think about the Seven Rs first.

❶ RETHINK

Do you really need to buy something new?

❷ REFUSE

Could you **Refuse** it instead? Such as saying "No thanks" to a free pen, when you have lots at home.

❸ REDUCE

Could you **Reduce** the number of new things you need to buy? Bring your own reusable drink bottle instead of buying new plastic ones.

If you really do have to buy something new, what should you do with it when you're finished?

4 REUSE

Could you **Reuse** it?
Such as reusing a plastic bottle as a watering can for your plants.

6 RECYCLE

Maybe you could **Recycle** it? Recycling means sending it to be made into something new. Such as cardboard being recycled into toilet paper.

If you can't refuse, reduce, reuse or repurpose, then you will have to throw it away.

5 REPURPOSE

Could you make a few changes and **Repurpose** it to use for something else? Such as turning an old t-shirt into a bag.

7 ROT IT DOWN

If it is plant-based, you could **rot it down**. Such as putting a banana peel into the compost.

23

"We have already made the leaves for our pledge tree, so it's too late to reduce or refuse the paper.

And I can't think of a way we can reuse or repurpose these little bits."

"Let's recycle them!"

Recycling bin

This is where we put waste that can be turned into something new, such as paper, glass, cardboard, and some plastics. The waste must be clean and dry so be sure to wash it first!

General waste bin

This is where we put anything that can't be recycled or put into the compost, like plastic that can't be recycled or cardboard that is wet or covered in food.

General waste gets sent to the landfill—a big area of land, which is used to dump trash. It can take thousands of years for trash in landfill to break down and it often releases lots of harmful chemicals.

Compost

This is where we put vegetable peelings and fruit waste.

We can be kind to the planet by carefully choosing which food to eat.

Hooray, it's lunch time! I grew the lettuce in my window box.

The strawberries came from a plant in my garden!

This honey came from my bees.

My neighbor's chickens laid these eggs.

Remind your grown-ups of "Pedro's golden rules for planet-friendly eating."

1. Try to pick food that is grown locally.
2. Try to avoid things with lots of packaging.
3. Try to eat less meat.

"Now that we are finished, we must remember to put our trash into the correct bins."

In many countries, nearly a third of all food is wasted.

"Paper, cardboard, and glass can all be easily recycled. Plastic can be much harder to recycle."

Our planet is very clever, it doesn't let anything go to waste. When plants and animals die, Earth has a way of recycling them.

Dung beetles carry away poop.

Millipedes and beetle grubs eat dead wood.

Carrion beetles eat dead animals.

Earth is very good at recycling natural materials, but it cannot recycle plastic.

All about plastic

Plastic is very useful. It's light, strong, and can be easily made into different shapes. However, it's not natural.

We can reuse and recycle some plastics but when we are finally finished with them our planet cannot recycle them into natural materials.

Plastic eventually breaks down into smaller and smaller pieces but this can take hundreds of years. The pieces make their way into the soil and the ocean.

If we don't stop creating so much plastic waste, there will soon be much more plastic in the ocean than fish.

Some plastic objects, such as water bottles, plastic bags, and packaging, are designed to only be used once. Try to avoid these types of plastic and instead...

Bring your own water bottle.

Bring your own bag.

Pick loose fruit and vegetables.

Scientists are researching new ways to break down plastic. One day, decomposers such as bacteria and fungi may help us to get rid of our plastic waste.

Time to head back outside.

 Switching off the electricity when we are not using it isn't just good for the planet, it can save money on energy bills too.

"These materials are left over from building the cabin. What could we make with this old bucket?"

"We could start a band?"

"Or play knights and dragons?"

"What about a bucket pond? It could provide a home for pond snails, pond skaters, and water beetles..."

"...and a drink for thirsty animals..."

"...and a bath for birds!"

"Great idea! Here's a good spot that's nice and flat, and out of the Sun."

First, we fill the bottom of the bucket with gravel and sand.

Then we add some larger rocks. They will make great hiding places for water bugs!

Finally, we add some recycled water.

This log will help any animals that fall in to crawl out again.

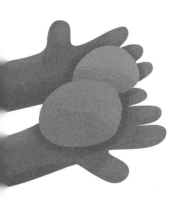

Finished! I wonder what creatures will move into the pond?

31

We are going to use this space to grow our own food from seeds.

You could grow your own food in a community garden, in a window box, or in your yard.

That worm is following us!

We have lots of seeds.

- ☑ Carrots
- ☑ Cucumbers
- ☑ Green beans
- ☑ Broccoli
- ☑ Beetroot
- ☑ Strawberries

First, we push our fingers into the soil to make little holes.

Then we put a seed in each hole...

...and cover them up with more soil.

Now we need to give them a big drink!

Use plastic bottles as watering cans and don't forget to use rainwater or leftover water.

The cabin is surrounded by green space. It makes me feel really calm.

Plants are constantly changing and growing —just like us!

Wild spaces look different depending on the weather and the season.

These are baby fruit trees. They will take many years to grow but one day they will produce tasty fruit to eat.

Baby trees are called saplings.

Trees are really important plants. They are helpful for people, animals, and the planet!

TREEMENDOUS TREES

Trees are tall plants with woody stems
that often live for a very long time.

Trees have been
around since the time
of the dinosaurs.

The oldest trees on
Earth are more than
5,000 years old.

Trees are very useful
to the planet.

They give out oxygen,
which humans and other
animals breathe.

They provide shade.

Their roots protect the soil
from being washed away.

They keep
our air clean.

"Before we head back, we are going to visit the oldest tree in the forest.

Isn't it beautiful?

If you sit at the base of its trunk and look up through its branches, you can see the clouds moving across the sky. They make all sorts of funny shapes."

"I can see a volcano.

What can you see?"

"I see a butterfly."

"I see a rabbit."

"I see a crow."

Never look at the Sun, as it's dangerous for your eyes.

Cutting down trees is also known as deforestation.

Some trees are grown to be cut down. These are often fast-growing types, such as spruces and firs.

WHY ARE TREES CHOPPED DOWN?

To make space...

To grow food for people.

To grow food for animals like sheep and cows.

To create roads.

We also dig in the ground under forests to create mines, where we can take out oil and metals.

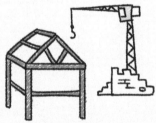

To build houses.

Planting new trees is a great way to help the planet!

Wood from the trees is used to make:
* Furniture
* Buildings
* Paper
* Clothing
* Firewood
* Charcoal.

"I planted some seeds here
earlier in the year. Now they
have grown into a wildflower
meadow. Look at all the insects!"

"They are feeding on
the flowers' nectar."

When insects visit flowers to drink
nectar, they also collect pollen,
which they take to other plants.
This is called pollination and
it helps make new plants.

"I can see lots of birds flying around too. They must be feeding on the insects."

AMAZING BUGS

Bugs are really important. They do lots of
jobs that keep our planet running as it should.

They clear up waste:

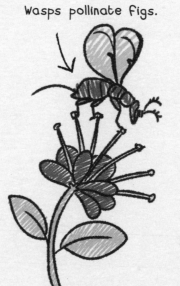

Termites eat rotting wood.

Flies eat poop.

They pollinate our plants, which helps make new plants:

Bees pollinate
strawberries.

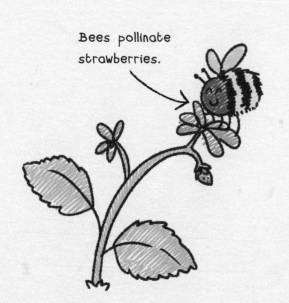

Wasps pollinate figs.

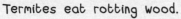

Butterflies
pollinate lavender.

They prepare the soil for plants:

Worms gobble up dead plants and poop out fertilizer (rich soil that helps plants grow).

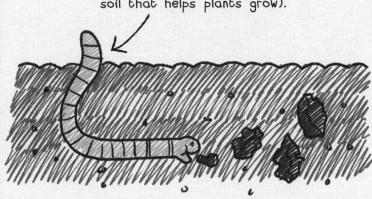

Millipedes tunnel through the soil, allowing rainwater to reach plant roots.

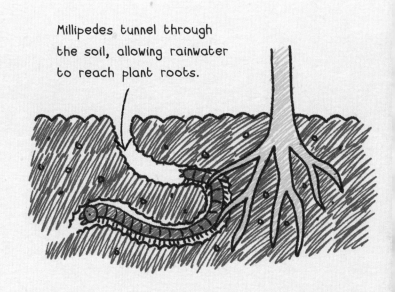

They provide food for birds and other animals:

Many birds feed caterpillars to their chicks.

Moles eat earthworms.

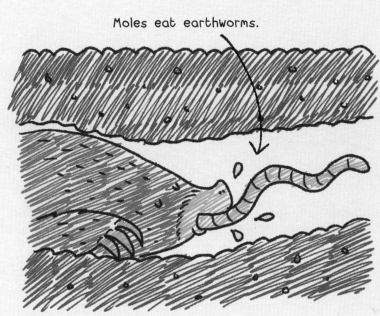

"Just one more thing to do before we go home...
...write our pledges!"

"I pledge to build a bucket
pond in my garden."

"I pledge to grow my
own strawberries."

"I pledge to always switch off the lights when I leave a room."

"I pledge to reuse water. What a great first day at the new eco cabin."

SWITCH **OFF** and **SAVE** ENERGY

We've stopped off at the community garden on our way home. Daniel works here with a group of volunteers. They grow fruit and vegetables.

The rhubarb is ready to harvest. It will make a delicious dessert!

'Let's carry the rhubarb home in a net bag, instead of a plastic one.'

I had such a wonderful day at the eco cabin. I learned that it's easy to make simple changes that can help to protect the planet.

What pledges will you make to help protect our planet? You'll be surprised how easy and fun being a planet hero can be!

HOW TO BE A
≡PLANET HERO≡

Isn't our planet amazing? There are no other planets we can move to if we ruin this one, so we must take good care of it. Every single thing that we do has an effect on our planet, so it's up to us to make sure the effect is a good one. Try the tips below to become a real-life PLANET HERO:

- Be careful not to waste water. Don't run the tap for longer than you need to and don't flush wet wipes down the toilet.

- Start a compost heap to rot down vegetable peelings and plant waste.

- Walk or cycle instead of using the car on short journeys.

- Talk to your friends about the problems the planet is facing, such as global warming and deforestation.

To protect all animals and the world they live in, it is also important to:

- Think carefully before buying new things. Try to avoid buying plastic and buy things second-hand whenever you can.

- Treat wild spaces with kindness, pick up any litter, stick to the paths, and never trample on plants or fungi.

- Grow green things wherever you can. Pack your windowsill with plants or create a vegetable patch.

Ava   Billy   Bella